W9-CMD-280

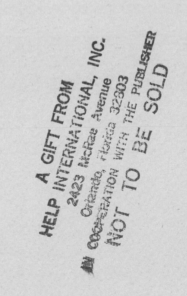

A GIFT FROM
HELP INTERNATIONAL, INC.
2423 McRae Avenue
Orlando, Florida 32303
IN COOPERATION WITH THE PUBLISHER
NOT TO BE SOLD

VANISHING BREED

VANISHING BREED

PHOTOGRAPHS OF THE COWBOY AND THE WEST

Photographs by William Albert Allard   Foreword by Thomas McGuane

A New York Graphic Society Book   Little, Brown and Company • Boston

Copyright © 1982 by William Albert Allard   Foreword copyright © 1982 by Thomas McGuane

All rights reserved. No part of this book may be reproduced in any form or by any electronic or mechanical means
including information storage and retrieval systems without permission in writing from the publisher, except by a
reviewer who may quote brief passages in a review.

Text and photographs on the following listed pages copyright © by National Geographic Society:
pp. 15, 18, 21, 26, 27, 30, 31, 36, 40, 42, 44, 48, 51, 59, 64, 65, 70, 91, 97, 107, 111, 114, 118, 123, 124, 136, 138, 139, 140.

Second printing, 1983

ISBN 0-8212-1505-1   0-8212-1524-8 (deluxe edition)   Library Of Congress Catalog No. 82-060768

New York Graphic Society books are published by Little, Brown and Company.
Published simultaneously in Canada by Little, Brown and Company (Canada) Limited.

Printed in Italy.

For my children — Scott, Chris, Terri, and David.
And for their mother, Katy.

FOREWORD

The West, whatever that is, is still there, believe it or not, in its entirety. It is the leading chimera of our geography. The dead windmills lost behind the high wire of a missile range, the stove-up old cowboy at the unemployment office, the interstate that plunges through the homesteads, all bring aches to an American race memory.

The demolition of the agrarian South by the industrial North in the Civil War was a precursor with similar power to generate ghosts, and to haunt with a mythology of disappearance.

The West vanished for the Indian and the drover; it vanished for the cowboy. Simultaneously it reappeared in all the same places, and in movies and rodeos. It's like fire. Hollywood, calf tables, and depreciation schedules can't kill it.

Images bombard us like flies on the windshield; the camera's power lies in specifics. The West is imbedded in a miasma of contradictory pictures. In William Allard we feel the power of search, like children rummaging through their grandparents' abandoned homes. It's not so much the trunks and old newspapers as it is the suspicion that the old people may still be alive, that what is lost is the connection. Exactly so are Americans lost with their own rootless drifting inside the boundaries of a continent.

We sense in these pictures not preservation — where would Allard put the deluded youths who mingle with his vanishing vaqueros? — but a true and moving quest to build a bridge that goes in two directions. For reasons of his own, the photographer seems happiest in a hard landscape, as it comes. His eye moves from those born to the West, to those who have learned it from scratch, to those who are on the run, and catches not only the sense of the land itself but the place as it is felt by those who live in it: a kind of borderless outpost.

Allard's photographs leave no footprints. Those subjects conscious of the process gaze at the camera as an indifferent object in a dimensional world. The viewer receives the same acceptance accorded a rock, a sandwash, a bar that is closed for repairs.

Conrad spoke of a shadow line, that faint demarcation between a world that is vanishing and another that is inexorably taking its place. In Allard's photographs we are moved by the feeling that no matter how thoroughly the vestigial society of a nearly open range is expelled, the world to come in this tremendous landscape will be shaped forever in memories, in legend, and in that transubstantial belief that one has been preceded by men in whom the sense of glory was not entirely diminished.

Thomas McGuane

PREFACE

This book is about a love affair with a place and its people. The place is immense — both grand and gritty — and in some ways as delicate as a flower. We call it the American West.

As with any affair of the heart, the words and images in this book represent a very personal viewpoint, and in this case are the result of pursuing the affair off and on over a period of about ten years, from Mexico to Canada.

The people in this book are mostly cowboys and others whose lives tend to reflect the traditional rural West. From the Mexican vaqueros, whose ancestors developed many of the skills used by American cowboys today, to Indian families on holiday in powwow lodges on a Montana reservation, to the plain-clothed Hutterites who first brought their communal life-style from Europe to a turn-of-the-twentieth-century West in search of a place to work and worship freely — all are people whose lives are tied by birth or choice to a part of America that just might prove to be the country's soul: a place where myth has long been in partnership with reality.

Many of the cowboys in this book are top hands who probably could have held their own and ridden with any outfit, in any era. But their replacements are not running around in bunches. One of our national myths is that the West is still filled with hard-riding cowboys pushing herds of cattle across the old purple sage. The reality, as any rancher will tell you, is that good working cowhands are getting harder and harder to find. According to a recent cattlemen's survey, there are now perhaps two thousand job openings for skilled cowboys throughout the West. The key word, of course, is *skilled.*

There are still a few big ranches today where a young man can hire on with the spring branding crew and ride long dusty days in the saddle gathering cattle that don't want to be gathered, doctoring cows that don't want to be doctored, wrestling and branding calves, and spending most of his nights sleeping on the ground until the wagon heads back in autumn. It's hard work. It can be boring. And it's lonely as hell if you don't like being alone. On a quarter-million-acre outfit it can take a couple of years just to learn the country, and a lot more than that to learn to think like a cow. But that's the traditional way to learn to be a cowboy. The skills don't automatically come with the boots and hat.

And once the cowboy has his skills mastered, they aren't really worth much, financially, when compared, for instance, to working in the mines or the oil fields. Cowboy wages today run from around four hundred to eight hundred dollars a month, with bed and board. During calving season on a cow-and-calf outfit that means working six weeks straight, seven days a week, twelve to fourteen hours a day — dawn to dark — riding the snow- and windswept drop pastures, and pulling calves from heifers in the calving barns, with sometimes precious little time to sit by the stove telling lies while the gloves dry.

Of course, most of the truly good hands aren't there for the money, anyway. They cowboy because they love the way of life and what comes with it: the freedom of space in country bigger than one's problems. True, you can't take that to the bank and make a deposit — but then, how many of us go to the bank or anywhere else nowadays with anything approaching comfort of mind?

For me, the West began to become a part of my consciousness as a child growing up in Minneapolis in the 1940s and early '50s. On our front porch were stacks of *The Saturday Evening Post,* their pages filled with illustrated stories about places with names like Broken Bow, Sweetwater, and the Bighorns. In those years, when a child's imagination was still nourished by magazines, books, and radio, rather than by television, those names always sounded right to me. There were stories of the sea as well, but for me it was always the mountains and the plains. I could see them in my mind.

Although raised in the city, I spent summers on a small Minnesota farm where I learned early the taste of well water and the sweet smell of horse sweat and fresh-cut hay. But that prairie-country farm was far different from the country I would come to know later. It wasn't until the mid-1960s that I first got a look at parts of western Wyoming and Montana. I can still remember one early morning in Wyoming and the first light on high mountain meadows touched by wisps of clouds within my reach. That first look demanded another, and another, until I found myself seeking any excuse, any story idea that would lead me back from the East, where I had moved, to that grand expanse of Wyoming or Nevada or Montana. Especially Montana. Perhaps only those who live there can fully appreciate that place and that space and what it can do for the soul. Just as perhaps only those who live in the West can really understand the penalty we will all pay if we fail to recognize that there can be no afterlife for a place that started out as heaven.

The images and the text vignettes in this book have been selected from work done in the West on a variety of assignments for various publishers over the years. Some of the text and the vast majority of the photographs have not been published previously. In retrospect, I suppose making some of the images in this collection was almost incidental to what I was really doing out there much of the time — just kind of trying to learn to be a cowboy. Can't say that I regret it.

I once knew an old hand, now no longer around, who used to muse about earlier times in Montana, when the country was more open, with fewer fences and gates to slow a man down — restrictions in the land of the free. I suppose we all feel more restricted today, regardless of our region. There seem to be gates in our lives that we never get open. But if we're lucky, we have a place, each of us, that is special. Others may see that place differently, of course. They can change it, and they probably will; they can even take it away. But if we love it deeply enough, there is a part of it within us to the end. I guess that's how I feel about this place we call the West. And that is why this book exists.

William Albert Allard
Mumps' Ha'
Barboursville, Virginia

Acknowledgments: Any list of acknowledgments can only end up incomplete. I would like, however, to mention a few of those who have been, in one way or another, a part of this work.

First and foremost: All of those who appear in words or pictures in this book. All the ranchers, cowboys, and buckaroos, who put up with me hanging around and never gave me any really bad horses. My friends among the Hutterite colonies of Montana, those wonderful people who embody the spirit of western hospitality, always offering food, friendship, song, and acceptance. Joe Redthunder of the Nez Percé, who carries on the traditions of his people in simple elegance of speech. Wind River Sally, as fine a dog as you could want, and a lot better looking than most. The drifters and the drinkers.

Among my colleagues: David Lyman, who convinced me it was time to let it go and move on. Jon Schneeberger, more than a friend and fine editor. R. Smith Schuneman, my first photography teacher, who long ago taught me discipline and respect for the profession. (He didn't say how hard it could be.) Sam Abell, James P. Blair, Susan Smith— always believers. Floyd Yearout of New York Graphic Society Books. And the National Geographic Society, for permission to publish work here that first appeared in their publications.

To all, I wish I could say something more than thank you.

VANISHING BREED

As for man, his days are as grass:
as a flower of the field, so he flourisheth.
For the wind passeth over it, and it is gone;
and the place thereof shall know it no more.

Psalms 103:15–16

Long ago, before the American Civil War, Mexican vaqueros perfected the art of roping horses and cattle. Their ropes were of braided rawhide, and their Corriente cattle were the forerunners of the Texas Longhorn. Their skills eventually passed on to the north, to the young Texas drovers who rode to the virgin grasslands of Kansas, Wyoming, and Montana.

18

A cowboy recalled the words of his father:

"Son, if you're going to be a cowboy, let me give you two pieces of advice:
Stick to herding steers – never work for a cow-and-calf outfit. And
never work for a man who has electricity in his barn. You'll be up all night."

Fifty-nine-year-old Vern Torrance leaned against a tent pole and rolled a cigarette. "I wish," he said, "that it was the end of this sonuvabitch — instead of just the beginning."

Not the least bit glamorous, branding is hard, sweaty work, wrestling calves that wear you out as they struggle in dust that chokes your breath. And in the coming weeks this crew would have to ride about forty-five thousand acres, gather three thousand cows, and brand their calves. It was, indeed, just the beginning.

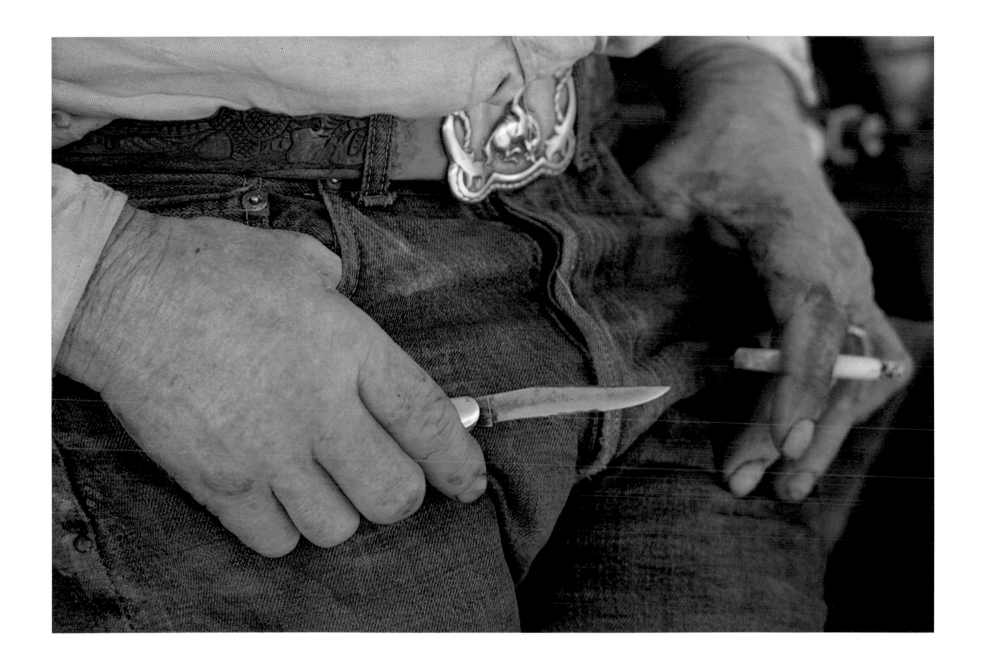

Brian Morris was a buckaroo for a big outfit in Nevada when I first met him.
"Buckaroo" is what a cowboy is called in that part of the country.
I spent some days out on the high deserts of Nevada with Brian — and a
few evenings in town, talking over drinks about cowboy life. I once said
to him, "Brian, the way everything is going, with more trucks, more fences,
more machines being brought in to do the job of a man with a rope and
a horse — do you think you'll ever be replaced by a machine?"

He looked at me and with his marvelous soft drawl he said, "Bill, they
just ain't come up with nothin' yet that'll take as much abuse as a cowboy."

The stubby remains of a Bull Durham smoke dangling from his lips,
he shook out a broad loop in his rope and slowly stalked across the dusty
corral, looking for a white-footed sorrel with a burr-tangled mane. The
horses eyed his approach and with ears flattened back suddenly whirled
away. The white-footed sorrel was buried deep among them as they
crowded wedgelike into a corner of the corral. There they stood with bodies
tensed, their heavily muscled hindquarters turned toward the man.
He closed a step or two. For a moment they held fast. Then, in an explosion
of pounding hooves and flashing legs, they came apart, some dashing
to the other end of the corral. For a second or two the sorrel was exposed.
He knew it and made his move. The cowboy made his. The horse
feinted left, then rolled back on his hocks and broke to the right. Swiftly,
smoothly, the cowboy cast the rope, his wrist turning downward at the
moment of release like a baseball pitcher throwing an overhand curve.
The open loop seemed to skim over the other horses by only inches and fell
softly on target. With a quick jerk, the man threw his weight behind the
rope and it made a zipping sound as the loop tightened around the sorrel's
neck. His role in the drama completed, the horse dropped his head
slightly in resignation, waiting to be led away.

The morning turned hot and the young hands were like athletes
struggling through the first day of training. Muscles quickly grew tired.
One calf wrestler had been bloodied from a kick in the jaw. Another had
been kicked in the groin and sat crumpled up against the fence like a pile
of dirty clothes, his head cradled in his arms.

We were headed back to the wagon by noon. Sweat lathered the necks
of our horses and they threw their heads nervously, bothered by the nose-
flies. Floyd looked over at a cowboy riding a flea-bit gray. "You know
something?" he said. "If we'd branded two hundred and seventy calves
today instead of just a hundred and seventy, it probably would've taken all
the fun out of it." Hungry, hot, and aching for a rest, the young man
silently looked at the wagon boss with eyes that were dust-rimmed and
weary. A big grin broke over Floyd's face as he tapped spurs to his bay
and we loped for camp, leaving tawny plumes of dust behind us.

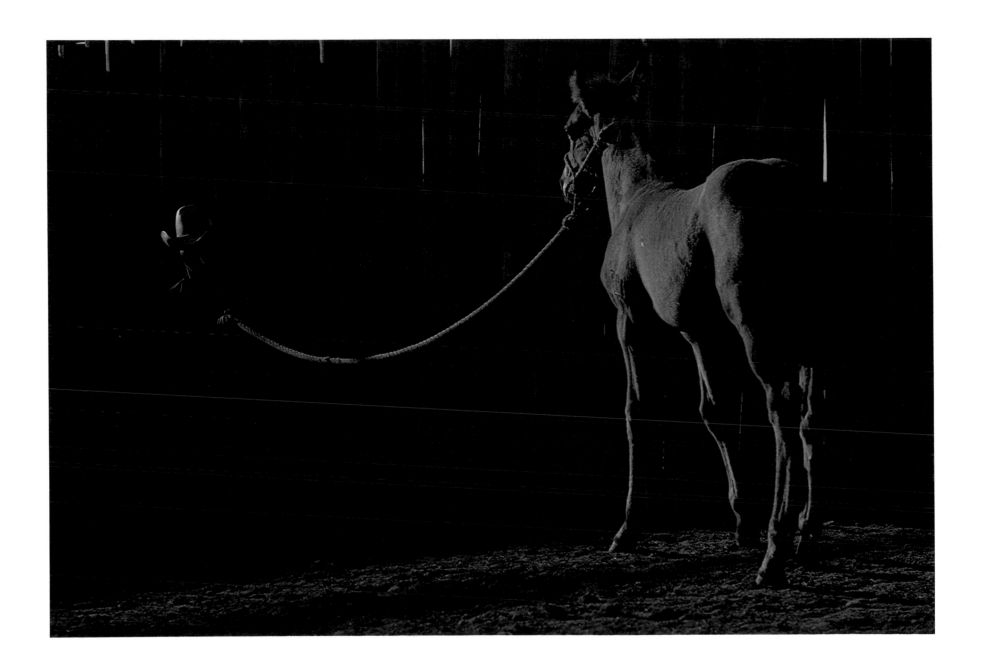

T.J. Symonds was about seventeen when I met him. He was from South
Dakota and he hadn't been doing too well at school or in staying out
of trouble. So his dad sent him down to Nevada to be a buckaroo.
And old T.J. was doing just fine as a buckaroo, except for his "heart attack."
It seems T.J. had been riding circle and found himself getting dizzy. He
managed to get off his horse before falling, but he was scared. Very
scared. Hank, the twenty-one-year-old cow boss, convinced that T.J. had
suffered a heart attack, rushed him by pickup truck to Elko, eighty-five
miles to the south. Not until reaching the emergency room did T.J. fully
regain consciousness, and in doing so, he looked up at the faces of
strangers clad in hospital white.
"Goddammit," he said, in despair, "I'm dead, ain't I? Dammit, I'm dead."
Well, he wasn't. Evidently T.J. had had some kind of heart flutter out
there on his horse, panicked, and as a result, hyperventilated — nothing
more serious than that. So he was released and advised to rest
for a day or so.
But you can't just turn loose a couple of young buckaroos in town —
especially when one of them is convinced he's just returned from the
dead — and expect them to go directly back out to the job. After all,
buckarooing isn't like a "real job." So, in traditional fashion, they made
the rounds: first stop was at Capriola's saddle shop for some new shirts
and hats, then on to the Commercial Hotel and the Stockmen's bar for
some drinks, and as dark closed on Elko, the final stop was at Mona's,
where the hours pass easy and the girls show a definite preference for
buckaroos over truck drivers and salesmen.

"I guess these boys don't know what it's like to work for a tough outfit," said Floyd Workman. "The horses here are pretty good, mostly broke before we get 'em. I've worked for outfits with trashy horses where the foreman tried to get you bucked off every morning. I guess it used to be fun watching the young hands gettin' bucked off them rank horses. Maybe that's why cowboys on rough outfits used to eat a light breakfast. I got so I couldn't eat breakfast. It was a low feeling in the morning worrying if you could cut it because if you didn't they'd put you to doin' somethin' else. I tell these kids that if they really want to punch cows in these hills, all they need is a good bed and a good saddle. You can take a pretty rough day if you've got a good bed. I don't mean one of them expensive sleepin' bags. Just a couple of blankets, maybe a piece of foam rubber, and a good canvas. Hell, a man can climb in according to the weather, put on top what he don't need underneath for a cushion. Sleepin' bag's either too hot or too cold, never seems just right. And then with a good saddle to ride, a man's ready to cowboy."

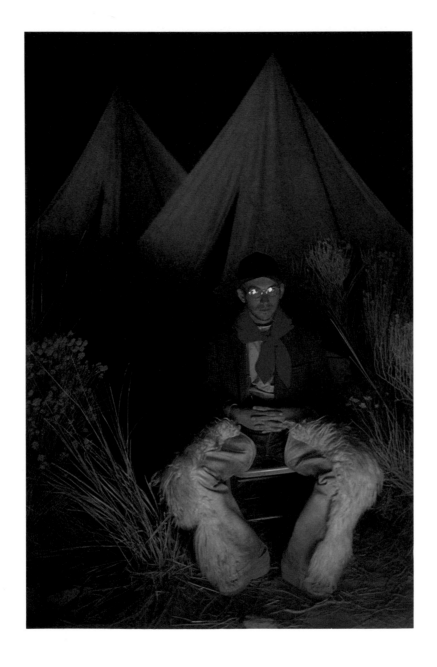

"A man I worked with on one outfit had a pair of bright orange wool chaps,"
Smitty recalled. "Orange woollies, they were. Another fella on the
outfit took a real likin' to those chaps. Decided he had to have 'em. Finally
traded the man for 'em. Gave him his wife and twenty-five dollars. He sure
liked them orange chaps."
My oldest son laughed at that story and probably thought Smitty had
made it up. Of course, my son has never seen a pair of orange woollies.
I saw a pair of green ones once, and they were beautiful.

"Goddamn! Did we get drunk last night? I woke up this morning and the door was open, the television set on, and the telephone hangin' down from the table. I don't know why that lady went home with me, drunk as I was."

Sid Wilson, age ninety-one, talked about breaking horses for the army
and riding in the Wild West shows.

"I'd spend the winters here, in Arizona," he said, "breaking horses for the
Spanish-American War. And in the summer I'd ride broncs for Buffalo
Bill's show. Old Buffalo Bill...he was a Christmas tree to everybody,
but he died busted.

"I started driving for the Sandy Bob Crouch stage line in Tombstone in
1906. The railroads had come in 1903 and taken over the mail contracts
and that was the end of the stagecoach. I used to drive a six-horse stage
from Tombstone to Benson and back, about a forty-mile round trip. It took
close to twelve hours, counting time to change horses. On June 30, 1906,
I drove the last stage to ever leave Tombstone."

Wilson was a rodeo cowboy for a few years after the stage stopped
running. Later he worked as a big-game guide and gathered wild horses in
Arizona and New Mexico. We sat in his ranch house in Tombstone.
He rolled a cigarette, and we looked at some scrapbooks with old and often
blurred photographs. He showed me pictures of horses that had died
years ago but whose names were fresh in his memory.

"Now there was a spinnin' sonuvabitch," he said, pointing out a picture
of himself on a rodeo bronc. "And there's little Gypsy Dog, mother
of old Pat. She was a fine horse."

He was a very interesting old man, who still rode and lived in the shadows
of his youth. He was still a cowboy.

Rodeo has always been touted as a haven for the last of the country's individualists. It's a sport that developed on the western frontier, where a man wasn't promised anything for his efforts. Not good weather, fair cattle prices, or getting back his entry fees. None of that has changed. In rodeo the luck of the draw can be almost as important as a cowboy's ability. In the bucking events both the cowboy and the animal are scored for their performance. It's not enough for a cowboy to simply stay aboard until the buzzer. A saddle bronc rider can rake his spurs from the break of the horse's shoulders all the way back to the cantle of the saddle in a perfect "lick" and do it all night long and still never see the pay window if the horse doesn't buck its best.

Rodeo, however, has always offered something besides money: independence — something we all would like to think we have and something the cowboy cherishes. To him, independence means being able to pick up his rigging and head on down the road for another shot at the big money and a championship belt buckle. A lot of them get down the road but damn few ever strap on the fancy buckle or win more than enough to pay expenses. But until a bronc falls on him in the chute or he gets hung up in his rigging or a bull hooks him so badly he'll never ride again — until then, the rodeo cowboy has got his independence.

"I wouldn't call it courage," said Doug Brown, 1969 World's Champion Bull-Rider. "There's no fear when they open that chute. If I look scared it's because I'm calling on my adrenalin and everything I've got inside of me to get up for the moment. It's not fear. Shit, if you're scared of the bulls you might as well go home. I've seen a few boys that were, but they didn't last long. Not that there aren't some things that frighten me. Hell, you couldn't melt me and pour me down a ski jump. No way."

During each performance a small and separate world exists behind the
chutes and in the dressing room. There, amid the backstage sounds
and smells of rodeo, the athletes in spurs and chaps congregate. Like
puppets on strings, the riders stand, twisting and jerking their bodies to
limber the muscles that will be put to a supreme test when the chute-
gates open. Behind the chutes is a place for trading encouragement and
advice on how to ride the animals each man has drawn for the night.
Littered with paper cups and cigarette butts, saddles and lumpy duffel bags,
it's a place where a cowboy can bum a chew of tobacco or
find out where the party will be later and where the girls are that are easy.
Constantly shattered by the sounds of heavy gates slamming shut
behind snorting horses that rear and kick against their steel enclosures,
it is a dust-covered world, pockmarked with spit.

With the blue coldness of dusk, the circle came to life. Families gathered
outside their tepees. A girl strolled by in a full-length buckskin dress,
her long black hair braided and wrapped in otter fur and red cloth. Pickup
trucks bumped along the road into the campground, headlights cutting
yellow shafts through a veil of dust. There were Indian crafts for sale,
and a white man set up a stand to sell balloons, key chains, neckerchiefs,
bumper stickers — the usual bright display of a powwow peddler.
And how much are the neckerchiefs? asked a young Indian.
''A dollar apiece, friend,'' said the huckster, ''and I've got all the pretty
colors. Red ones, blue ones…you want a red one?''
''Hell, yes, I want a red one,'' said the young man. ''I ain't a blue Indian.''
From a large, open-sided tent came the hollow echoing
of drums. Dogs barked.

When America was young and innocent, before white men came with
their books, their missionaries, and a hunger for land, Indian children
learned many things through the imagery of legends. From the adventures
of Coyote, Fox, and Grizzly Bear, they learned the virtues of
bravery and honor, and the tragedy of greed. Around the warmth
of winter fires they heard about the mysteries of plants and animals and the
sacredness of Mother Earth. And in one of the most ancient legends
they learned that Coyote had once predicted the coming of a "new age" —
the time of "human beings." With that age, he had said, would come
struggle to overcome sorrow.

The whispers of the stream seemed to echo the words of a young man
I'd met who had left New York to become a cowboy. "What I like best
about this country," he had said, "is that if I'm mad at something or get
to hating somebody, I can go out alone on a ridge or down along a winding
creek and forget about it all."

From the branches of an ash tree a red-winged blackbird sent out high,
thin, single notes. Humming insects swarmed around cattails that parted
the water in murmured ripples. From somewhere on the opposite bank
something entered the stream with a soft splash and horses coming
down to water nickered low in their throats at the faint rumble of
distant thunder.

"I worked for an outfit up on the Musselshell when I was just a kid," said Tom Roberson, an eighty-eight-year-old Montanan. "Two men came into our roundup camp one evening, riding the best saddle horses I'd ever seen. I guess I was the only one in camp that didn't know them. One of 'em came over to me and said, 'Hey, kid, I'm out of a bed, but I'm clean. How's chances of bunkin' with you?' I had a new bedroll and I said, 'Sure – but you take those spurs off, because if you tear my new blankets I'll never forgive you.' He took his boots off and laid down with his six-shooter right next to him.

"Come morning, he gave me a gold ring. 'Here, kid,' he said, 'keep this to remember the night you slept with a train robber.' The cook gave 'em a sack of biscuits, boiled meat, and some coffee, and they rode off without another word. It was Kid Curry and his brother. They'd robbed a train and were getting out of the country as fast as they could, leaving as few tracks as possible. You know, if the law had come along, they wouldn't have learned a thing from our bunch. That was the custom of the country.

"Yes," Tom Roberson said, "I have ridden with a few men who lived outside the law. And I won't say how law-abiding I might have been myself. It was raw country then. I've taken horses that weren't mine and used 'em as long as I wanted to. But I never did steal a horse. Always turned it loose when I got done with it."

He showed me a beautiful pair of spurs he'd made with hammered silver on the shanks. I offered to buy them. "I'd kind of hate to sell my last pair of spurs," he said. "It would be like saying good-bye."

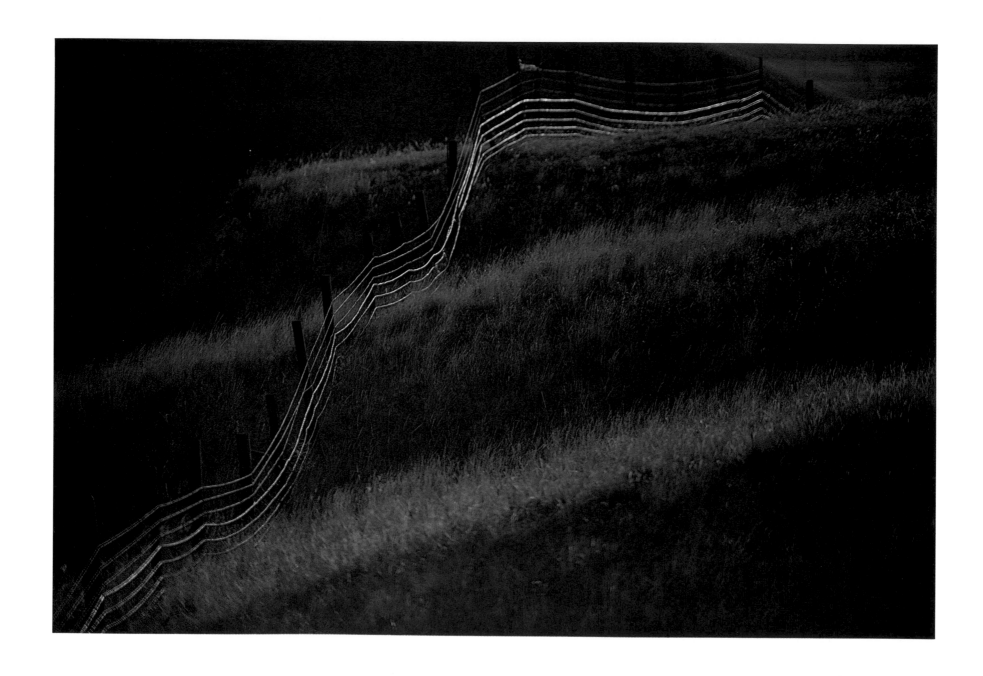

120

In an old frame ranch house the bedrolls of a half dozen Nevada buckaroos lay scattered about like abandoned cocoons. We'd finished off a lot of whiskey, and the empty bottles stood glistening on a table beneath the pale, hissing light of a gas lantern. Nate Morris sat at the table in his long underwear. Almost sixty, he could still ride well enough to run down a mustang. In a voice husky from age and booze and not enough sleep, he sang old cowboy songs about wild horses and the men who rode them — songs about strawberry roans and wild-eyed stallions. Old Nate...that was more than ten years ago, but I can still remember the sound of his voice.

It started to snow the night before we were to trail a thousand steers twelve miles to the shipping pens. The first flakes melted quickly, becoming dirty streaks on the windowpanes. Outside the door, Butch's cow dog Bill whimpered to be let in. Jim Martin walked out to see if the sky might clear. When he returned I asked how he thought the weather would be by morning.

"Deep and still," he said slowly in his high-pitched Texas accent.

"What's *that* mean?" I asked.

"Deep as your ass and still snowing," he replied.

We rode along the Middle Fork of Utah's Ogden River. As we picked our
way through groves of silver-gray cottonwoods and clumps of red-limbed
willows, an afternoon snow shower brought huge flakes that caught
the sun and fell like shining nickels. We tied our horses to scrub oaks near
a beaver dam. Yellow chips were scattered around a cottonwood
stump. Willows at the pond's edge had been stripped of bark.

"If you're gonna be a trapper, it helps to have a good wife," said Bruce,
looking for a trap he'd set the day before. "My wife comes out and helps
me sometimes. Once we had a bobcat caught up on a log above a
creek. She climbed out on the log with me and fell right in the creek.
God, it was funny! But I knew it weren't no time to laugh."

Bruce finally located the wire leading to the trap, which a beaver had
dragged beneath an ice ledge hanging over the pond. He tugged futilely at
the wire running into the water; then, rolling up his sleeves, and
without the benefit of rubber waders, he walked slowly into the pond.
The water was hip-deep and breathtakingly cold.
He lowered his head into the water to look beneath the ice and reached
under with his arms to pull and jerk at the wire. Finally it gave, and in his
raw, red hands he held a large, darkly glistening drowned beaver. Bruce
skinned the carcass and draped the shiny pelt across the cantle of his
saddle. We headed downriver. "Sometimes it's a pretty good living,
sometimes it ain't too much," he said. "Just like any other small business,
I suppose. But I guess I'd rather take a few dollars off the mountain
than to be punching a clock every day."

"When I was a kid they used to trail steers from Dillon to Salt Lake for nine dollars a head. The drive took over two weeks. Nine dollars a head!

Hell, I can remember working for twelve dollars a month, ten hours a day, including Sundays. But in those days I could buy work socks for three cents a pair, two pair for a nickel.

"I saw the last man hanged in Bannack," said Fritz. "Dad used to sell cheese there and I'd go with him and we'd sleep in the wagon so's nobody would steal the cheese. One afternoon some kids told me there was a man in town dressed just like a bird. I ran downtown with 'em. A gold robber had been tarred and feathered, and people was throwin' eggs and tomatoes at him. They was about to hang him behind the courthouse from a tripod of poles. They made him stand on top of two fifty-gallon beer barrels stacked end to end. Had quite a time getting him up there.

Then they put the rope around his neck. There must of been five hundred people watching.

"Anyway, some fella in the crowd says, 'Have you got anything to say?' The man didn't say anything. Somebody else shouts, 'If you ain't gonna say nothing, say so!' Well, we waited — must of been two, three minutes. Finally, he says, 'When I'm dead, bury me on my face.' Someone in the crowd says, 'What's that for?' And the man says, 'So all my friends can kiss my ass.' They kicked over the barrels and down he went. He was a brave sonuvabitch."

That's how seventy-six-year-old Fritz Waukley remembered it.

There had been no rain for weeks, and though we walked our horses, the
sun brought sweat to their withers. The seventeen-year-old Hutterite
boy from the Surprise Creek colony near Stanford, Montana, told me that
you can tell it's really dry when a single rider can kick up a dust trail.
We stopped at a stream. The water we drank had come down from the
mountains, and it was cool and tasted of the earth. In the thick heat of
midday we drank carelessly, splashing our faces until our shirtfronts
hung wet and the falling droplets made pockmarks in the dust.
"Do you ever feel like going away?" I asked.
"What do you mean?" he said.
"You know – do you ever feel like leaving the colony?"
"No," he said. "I've never felt a temptation to leave here. It must be a
pretty rough life on the outside, all alone, trying to make a living.
Don't you think?"
We let the horses drink and then rode on.
"Yes," I told him. "It can be all of that."

In the willows by the creek I saw a rabbit and it saw me and stopped, its
    velvet body frozen in anticipation, unsure of my intent. "Have you ever
tried to tame a wild rabbit?" an Indian friend had asked me miles ago. "It
    may seem yours for a while and then one day it flees if it can or if it can't
then it dies because it willed itself to die. They must be free. That is the
    way of wild things."
Yes. And man must also be free. Not because he is wild, but because he is
    capable of reason and can, if he chooses, will himself to live and grow
with humanity, and to the earth renew his dedication.
The rabbit, its eyes like liquid sensors, watched intensely as I moved
    slowly along a path that would cross the creek and take me away from
that place.
    I looked back a moment later, and it was gone.

PHOTOGRAPHS

Edited by Floyd Yearout   Copyedited by Michael Brandon   Designed by Carl Zahn   Production coordinated by Nan Jernigan

Typeset in *Serifa* by Typographic House, Inc., Boston, Massachusetts

Printed and bound by Arnoldo Mondadori Editore, Verona, Italy